The Sun is Up

by Claire Llewellyn   illustrated by Ayesha Lopez

 CAMBRIDGE UNIVERSITY PRESS  Institute of Education

The sun shines on the sea.

The sun shines on the trees.

The sun shines on the farm.

The sun shines on the pond.

The sun shines on the town.

The sun shines on the house.

The sun shines on me!

The Sun is Up ✦ Claire Llewellyn

Teaching notes written by Sue Bodman and Glen Franklin

Using this book

Developing reading comprehension

Even though this simple explanatory text uses a repeated sentence structure, it is a non-literal meaning. When using this book, children need to be guided to the understanding that it is not the sun itself that is on the landscape, but its rays. This is supported by the illustrations throughout and it would be helpful to guide children to look at where the rays of sunlight are falling in order to gather information on the storyline.

Grammar and sentence structure

- One simple repeated sentence structure.
- Text is well-spaced to support the development of one-to-one correspondence.
- In contexts where children are learning English as an additional language, support by rehearsing the sentence structure orally before introducing the book.

Word meaning and spelling

- Rehearse blending easy to hear sounds into a familiar word 'sun'.
- Reinforce recognition of frequently occurring words 'The', 'on', 'the'.

Curriculum links

Science - This book provides useful links with the topic of the weather. The illustrations show the sun at different times of the day. This could be linked to science activities which chart the progression of the sun's rays during the day. The final page could be used to begin discussion on the harmful effects of the sun on skin.

Other Pink A texts in this series can be used to develop one-to-one correspondence.

Learning outcomes

Children can:

- demonstrate early book-handling skills
- understand that left page comes before right
- understand that print is read from left to right
- start to match spoken word to printed word (one-to-one correspondence) and confirm this matching using a few known words or letters
- work out the storyline by gathering information from the illustrations and repeated language patterns.

A guided reading lesson

Introducing the text

Give a book to each child and read the title to them.

Orientation

Orient the children the book, using the verb in the same form as it is in the text:

Give a brief overview of the text: *This book is called 'The Sun is Up'. We will see how on a sunny day, the sun shines on everything. We're going to look at the pictures and talk about the book first, and then you can read it by yourself.*

Preparation

Page 2: *'The sun shines on the sea.' How do we know that the sun shines on the sea? Is there something in the picture to help us? Let's all read together, pointing to each word as we go 'The sun shines on the sea.'.* Support if necessary.

Page 5: *Now where is the sun shining? How do we know it is the farm?*

Page 14: *Where is the sun shining now? What does the little girl say?* (suggest *'The sun shines on me.'* if children do not) *Check that, point with your finger as you read. Where we right?*